Delivering Negative Feedback with Empathy and Effectiveness

Giving and Receiving Feedback for Success

Ben Sorensen

Published by Ben Sorensen, 2024.

While every precaution has been taken in the preparation of this book, the publisher assumes no responsibility for errors or omissions, or for damages resulting from the use of the information contained herein.

DELIVERING NEGATIVE FEEDBACK WITH EMPATHY AND EFFECTIVENESS

First edition. November 16, 2024.

Copyright © 2024 Ben Sorensen.

Written by Ben Sorensen.

BEN SORENSEN

Also by Ben Sorensen

Giving and Receiving Feedback for Success
Delivering Negative Feedback with Empathy and Effectiveness
Negative Feedback: Dealing with it and Growing from it

Watch for more at
bensorensen1.com/books

An Informal Introduction

In my previous book, *Negative Feedback: Dealing with it and Growing from it*, we unpacked being on the receiving end of negative feedback, and after much feedback, both positive and negative, I thought it time to write a book on the other part of that difficult conversation, delivering negative feedback.

Through this book, and in a perfect world, both books, I'm hoping to positively alter the dynamics, improve meaningful communication, and drastically increase personal growth, resolution of issues, and the complex social tapestry in which we live.

As always, this is designed to give you tips, help you understand the mechanics, and present your information in the best way possible – constructively and with empathy.

At the end of this book, I've included a list of resources I used in my research, that I also suggest as further reading if you want to delve deeper.

I hope this aids in your understanding and helps reduce the stress that comes from delivering negative feedback, and how its received.

Ben

Chapter 1

The Art of Constructive Criticism

How can you deliver feedback in a way that inspires, rather than discourages?

Providing negative feedback is a delicate art that requires striking the right balance between honesty and empathy. Constructive criticism should motivate the recipient to improve while maintaining their dignity and self-worth. In this chapter, we explore the fundamentals of delivering feedback that is clear, actionable, and encouraging, ensuring that your message fosters growth rather than resentment or discouragement.

Constructive criticism is feedback intended to help someone improve by providing specific, actionable insights. Unlike harsh or judgmental criticism, constructive criticism focuses on the behaviour or action rather than attacking the person. When delivered effectively, it can be a powerful tool for growth and learning.

Psychologist **B.F. Skinner's** research on reinforcement and feedback in the mid-20th century highlights the importance of feedback in behaviour change. Constructive criticism aligns with the principles of positive reinforcement, where highlighting desired outcomes and providing clear paths for improvement can significantly boost performance.

The Benefits of Constructive Criticism

1. **Promotes Growth**: When individuals receive actionable feedback, they are more likely to identify areas for improvement and take steps to enhance their skills or behaviour.

2. **Fosters Stronger Relationships**: Delivering feedback with kindness and respect can build trust and strengthen relationships, whether in personal or professional settings.

3. **Encourages Open Communication**: Constructive feedback can promote a culture of openness and continuous improvement, where people feel safe to share ideas and concerns.

Core Principles of Effective Constructive Criticism

1. **Focus on Behaviour, Not the Person** One of the most important principles of constructive criticism is to target the specific behaviour or action, rather than making generalized or personal comments about the individual. This approach helps to depersonalize the feedback, making it easier for the recipient to accept and act on it.
    - *Ineffective*: "You are always so lazy with your projects."
    - *Effective*: "I noticed that the last project was submitted late, which affected the team's timeline. Let's discuss how we can manage deadlines more effectively in the future."

2. **Be Specific and Objective** Vague feedback leaves people confused about how to improve. Instead, focus on providing concrete examples and objective observations.
    - *Vague*: "Your presentation was bad."
    - *Specific*: "Your presentation could be improved by adding more data to support your arguments and speaking more slowly to ensure everyone can follow along."

3. **Use "I" Statements** When delivering feedback, use "I" statements to express how the behaviour impacted you or the project, rather than placing blame on the person.
    - *Blaming*: "You didn't care about the meeting agenda."
    - *Empathetic*: "I felt that the meeting would have been more effective if we had followed the agenda closely. What can we do next time to make that happen?"

4. **Balance the Negative with the Positive** A well-known technique is the **feedback sandwich**, where you start with a positive comment, deliver the constructive criticism in the middle, and end with another positive note. While some criticize this method as predictable or insincere, it can be effective when used thoughtfully.

- *Example*: "Your dedication to the project has been incredible. One thing I'd like to discuss is the way we handle client communications, as I think there's room for improvement. Overall, your leadership has made a significant impact on the team."

Techniques for Delivering Constructive Criticism

1. **Timing is Key** Choose the right moment to deliver feedback. Criticizing someone in front of their peers can lead to embarrassment, while waiting too long to address an issue can make the feedback irrelevant. Aim to provide feedback soon after the event, but not when emotions are running high.

2. **Practice Active Listening** Constructive criticism should be a two-way conversation. Give the recipient a chance to express their thoughts and feelings and listen actively to understand their perspective. This approach fosters mutual respect and opens the door for meaningful dialogue.

3. **Offer Solutions and Support** It's not enough to point out what went wrong. Offering potential solutions or asking how you can support the recipient in improving can make your feedback far more constructive and actionable.
    - *Example*: "I noticed that you've been struggling with meeting deadlines. Would a weekly check-in help us track progress better? I'm here to support you in any way that I can."

4. **Maintain a Calm and Respectful Tone** Your tone can greatly impact how your feedback is received. Keep your voice calm and ensure your body language conveys openness rather than hostility. Even when discussing difficult topics, maintaining respect is essential.

Imagine you are a manager giving feedback to a team member whose performance has been inconsistent. An ineffective approach would be to accuse them of being unreliable, which could make them defensive. Instead, you could say:

DELIVERING NEGATIVE FEEDBACK

"I've noticed that your project updates have been delayed a few times recently, which has impacted our team's workflow. Is there anything I can do to help you manage your workload more effectively?"

This approach shows that you are focused on the specific behaviour (late updates) and are offering support rather than making the person feel attacked. By using constructive criticism, you create a space for dialogue and problem-solving.

Mastering the art of constructive criticism is a skill that can transform relationships and improve outcomes in various areas of life. By focusing on behaviour, being specific, and balancing feedback with kindness and support, you can deliver criticism that inspires growth rather than resistance. As we move through the rest of the book, you'll gain more tools to ensure your feedback has a positive, lasting impact.

Chapter 2

Understanding the Emotional Impact

Feedback can evoke strong emotions.

Giving and receiving feedback isn't just about communication skills; it involves complex emotional and psychological reactions. Criticism, no matter how well-intentioned, can sometimes trigger defence mechanisms, feelings of inadequacy, or even a complete shutdown of communication. In this chapter, we explore why feedback can provoke such strong emotions, how our brains are wired to process criticism, and strategies to mitigate emotional fallout when delivering feedback.

The Psychology Behind Feedback Reactions

The Brain's Defence Mechanisms

When we receive feedback, particularly negative feedback, our brain often perceives it as a threat. The **amygdala**, a part of the brain involved in emotional processing, is triggered in a reaction commonly known as the **fight-or-flight response**. This is the same response that is activated in situations of physical danger, causing an immediate emotional reaction that can make it difficult to process feedback constructively.

According to research in **neuroscience**, the brain tends to perceive social threats, such as criticism or rejection, as seriously as physical threats. **David Rock's SCARF Model** outlines five social domains that activate threat and reward responses: Status, Certainty, Autonomy, Relatedness, and Fairness. Feedback can threaten a person's sense of status or certainty, leading to defensive behaviour.

Why Criticism Hurts So Much

Humans are naturally sensitive to social evaluations. The **Negativity Bias**, a well-documented psychological phenomenon, suggests that people are more affected by negative experiences than by positive ones. Thus, negative feedback tends to have a more profound emotional impact than positive feedback. Understanding this bias helps us appreciate why people often dwell on criticism and may have strong, adverse reactions to it.

Dr. John Gottman's research on relationships found that it takes five positive interactions to counteract the emotional impact of a single negative interaction. This "5:1 ratio" is crucial to keep in mind when delivering feedback to ensure it is balanced with enough positive reinforcement.

Common Emotional Reactions to Feedback

1. **Defensiveness** People often become defensive when their self-concept is challenged. Defensiveness can manifest as arguing, denying, or shifting blame. It's a natural response aimed at protecting one's ego.
    - *Example*: An employee who receives criticism about their work quality might respond by listing reasons why the project was difficult rather than acknowledging the feedback.
2. **Shame and Embarrassment** Criticism can trigger feelings of shame, particularly if the person has a perfectionist mindset or struggles with self-esteem. Shame can make people feel unworthy or inadequate, which can hinder their ability to reflect on the feedback constructively.

Brené Brown's research on vulnerability emphasizes the importance of handling shame with care. Her work shows that when people experience shame, they are less likely to change and more likely to hide or become defensive.

3. **Anxiety and Stress** For some, the anticipation of feedback can be anxiety-inducing, especially if they have had negative experiences with criticism in the past. Anxiety can cloud judgment and make it difficult to process the feedback rationally.
    - **Practical Tip**: Address feedback anxiety by setting clear expectations and providing a supportive environment. When people know what to expect and feel respected, their anxiety is reduced.

How to Mitigate Emotional Reactions When Giving Feedback

1. **Acknowledge Emotions First** If you sense that the recipient is becoming defensive or emotional, take a moment to acknowledge their feelings. Simple statements like, "I understand that this might be difficult to hear," can go a long way in diffusing tension.

2. **Use Empathetic Communication** Empathy means recognizing and validating the other person's emotions. Rather than dismissing their reaction, show that you care. This doesn't mean sugarcoating the message but delivering it with consideration for how it may be received.
    - *Example*: Instead of saying, "This needs to change," try, "I can see you've worked hard on this. Here's something that I think could improve your results even more."

3. **Provide Context and Clarify Intentions** Explain why you're giving feedback and what your intentions are. Making it clear that your goal is to help, not to criticize for the sake of criticizing, can reduce the perceived threat.
    - *Example*: "I'm sharing this feedback because I believe in your potential and want to help you grow."

The Role of Self-Awareness in Feedback Reactions

Self-awareness plays a crucial role in how we process feedback. **Emotional intelligence** expert **Daniel Goleman** suggests that being aware of our emotional triggers can help us manage our reactions. People who are more self-aware can separate their sense of self-worth from the critique and view feedback as an opportunity for improvement rather than a personal attack.

Self-Reflection Strategies

1. **Journaling**: Writing down emotional reactions to feedback can help process feelings and identify patterns in responses.

2. **Mindfulness Practices**: Techniques such as deep breathing or meditation can help regulate emotional responses and bring a sense of calm to high-stress situations.

3. **Seeking Support**: Talking about feedback with a trusted friend or mentor can help put it into perspective and provide emotional reassurance.

Consider a situation where a manager has to deliver negative feedback to an employee who tends to get defensive. Instead of jumping straight into the critique, the manager could start by saying:

"I'd like to have a constructive conversation about some areas where we can make improvements. I want to emphasize that my goal is to support your growth, not to criticize. Let's work through this together."

By framing the feedback in a supportive context and showing empathy, the manager reduces the likelihood of a defensive reaction. The employee is more likely to engage in a constructive dialogue, leading to better outcomes.

Understanding the emotional impact of feedback is crucial for delivering it effectively. By recognizing common reactions, acknowledging emotions, and using empathetic communication, you can ensure your feedback is received in the spirit it is intended. The next chapter will explore practical strategies for preparing yourself for difficult feedback conversations, equipping you with the tools to manage your own and others' emotions.

Chapter 3

Preparing Yourself

Self-awareness is key to effective feedback.

The success of any feedback exchange is heavily influenced by how well you, as the feedback giver, are prepared. Emotional and mental preparation helps ensure that the conversation is constructive, empathetic, and goal-oriented. Before addressing another person's behaviour or performance, taking a moment to reflect, strategize, and regulate your emotions can make all the difference.

The Importance of Self-Preparation

Giving feedback isn't just about what you say but how you say it and the mindset you bring to the conversation. According to **psychologist Daniel Goleman's work on emotional intelligence**, self-regulation is one of the most crucial skills for leaders and individuals who frequently engage in feedback conversations. Self-regulation involves the ability to manage your emotions and stay calm and collected, even in challenging situations.

Preparation helps you:

1. **Clarify Your Intentions**: What do you hope to achieve with this feedback? If your goal is to help the person improve rather than criticize, your delivery will reflect that positive intent.

2. **Stay Focused on the Issue**: Preparing in advance allows you to identify and stick to the specific behaviours or outcomes you want to address, reducing the likelihood of straying into unrelated territory.

3. **Remain Calm and Objective**: Taking time to prepare helps you manage your emotions, ensuring that you don't react impulsively or let frustration guide your words.

Steps for Preparing Yourself

1. Clarify Your Intentions

Before delivering feedback, ask yourself:

- *What is my purpose in giving this feedback?*
- *Am I genuinely interested in helping the person improve?*
- *How will this feedback benefit the person or the team?*

Intent matters. Feedback given out of frustration or annoyance will come across as harsh or judgmental, even if you don't mean it that way. Clear intentions set the tone for a constructive conversation.

Case Study: Consider a manager who is upset about a missed deadline. If the manager confronts the employee without first calming down and reflecting, the conversation might become accusatory. By preparing and focusing on the impact of the missed deadline rather than the frustration, the manager can guide the conversation toward solutions.

2. Regulate Your Emotions

It's natural to feel emotional when someone's actions have disappointed or frustrated you. However, bringing those emotions into a feedback conversation can be counterproductive. Here are some techniques for emotional regulation:

1. **Take Deep Breaths**: Simple breathing exercises can help lower your heart rate and calm your nervous system.
2. **Delay the Conversation if Necessary**: If you're feeling highly emotional, it's okay to take a step back and revisit the conversation later. However, don't delay so long that the feedback loses relevance.
3. **Practice Self-Reflection**: Ask yourself what about the situation is making you emotional. Understanding your triggers can help you respond more thoughtfully.

Research Insight: Studies in **emotional regulation**, such as those by Dr. James Gross at Stanford University, have shown that people who practice techniques like reappraisal (reframing the situation in a more positive light) are more successful at staying composed in stressful interactions.

3. Gather Facts and Specific Examples

Vague or generalized feedback often leaves the recipient confused or defensive. Preparing specific examples and data points ensures that your feedback is grounded in reality rather than perception.

- *Ineffective*: "You're not contributing enough."
- *Effective*: "In the last two team meetings, I noticed that you didn't share any input during our brainstorming sessions. Your insights are valuable, and I'd love to hear your ideas more often."

Preparation Tip: Write down key examples before the meeting. This ensures you have evidence to support your points and helps structure the conversation more effectively.

4. Anticipate Reactions

Consider how the recipient might react to your feedback. Are they likely to be defensive, emotional, or open? Preparing for potential reactions allows you to respond calmly and empathetically.

- **Defensive Reaction**: If you think the person might become defensive, plan how to stay composed and redirect the conversation.
- **Emotional Reaction**: Be ready to show empathy and give the person space to process their emotions.

Empathetic Approach: "I understand that this feedback might be difficult to hear. Take your time to process it, and we can discuss any concerns you have."

5. Practice Your Delivery

Rehearsing what you plan to say can help you feel more confident and ensure that your message comes across as intended. Practice in front of a mirror or with a trusted friend. Focus on:

- **Tone of Voice**: Your tone should be calm, respectful, and neutral.
- **Body Language**: Maintain open and non-threatening body language, such as uncrossed arms and eye contact.

Communication Expert Insight: Dr. Albert Mehrabian's studies on communication show that nonverbal cues (body language and tone) account for a significant portion of how messages are received. Ensuring that your nonverbal cues align with your verbal message is crucial.

Mindset Matters: Cultivating a Growth-Oriented Approach

Approaching feedback with a **growth mindset**, a concept popularized by psychologist **Carol Dweck**, can transform how you deliver and perceive feedback. A growth mindset views challenges and feedback as opportunities to learn and grow rather than threats. When you communicate from this perspective, you're more likely to inspire positive change.

Self-Talk Before Feedback

Before engaging in a feedback conversation, use positive self-talk to remind yourself of your purpose:

- "I'm here to help this person improve."
- "This conversation is an opportunity for growth for both of us."

Real-World Example: A Difficult Feedback Situation

Imagine you're a teacher who needs to address a student's disruptive behaviour in class. Instead of confronting the student impulsively, you take time to prepare. You remind yourself of your goal: to help the student understand the impact of their behaviour and encourage them to participate positively.

During the conversation, you maintain a calm tone, provide specific examples of the behaviour, and ask for the student's perspective. Your preparation makes the conversation more productive, and the student feels respected rather than reprimanded.

Preparation is the cornerstone of effective feedback delivery. By clarifying your intentions, regulating your emotions, gathering facts, and practicing your delivery, you can transform potentially difficult conversations into opportunities for growth and connection. In the next chapter, we'll discuss how to create a supportive environment for feedback conversations, further enhancing the impact of your words.

Chapter 4

Creating a Supportive Environment

Feedback is most effective in a context of trust and mutual respect.

Feedback is not delivered in a vacuum; the environment in which it is given can make or break its effectiveness. Creating a space where people feel safe and supported to give and receive feedback is a critical component of healthy communication, whether in the workplace, a classroom, or at home. This chapter delves into how to cultivate a culture of trust, safety, and respect to maximize the positive impact of your feedback.

Why Environment Matters

Studies in **organizational psychology** emphasize that the physical and psychological environment influences how feedback is received and acted upon. When people feel threatened or judged, their ability to engage meaningfully in a conversation diminishes. Conversely, when they feel respected and safe, they are more open to reflection and change.

Edgar Schein, a renowned expert in organizational culture, noted that psychological safety is essential for learning and innovation. A feedback-rich culture, Schein argues, thrives when individuals believe they can voice concerns or hear constructive criticism without fear of humiliation or retaliation.

Key Elements of a Supportive Environment

1. Psychological Safety

Creating psychological safety means ensuring that people feel safe to take interpersonal risks. In a psychologically safe environment, individuals know that they won't be punished or ridiculed for admitting mistakes, asking questions, or receiving constructive criticism.

Amy Edmondson, a leading researcher on psychological safety, discovered through her studies at Harvard that high-performing teams are not necessarily the most technically skilled but are the ones where members feel safe to be vulnerable and candid. For example, Google's **Project Aristotle** found that psychological safety was the most important factor contributing to a team's success.

Practical Strategies for Fostering Psychological Safety:

- **Be Open and Transparent**: Explain why feedback is important and what you hope to achieve from the conversation.

- **Encourage Vulnerability from Leaders**: When leaders admit their own mistakes and model how to handle feedback well, it creates a norm for others to follow.

- **Acknowledge and Validate Feelings**: Simple statements like, "I understand this may feel uncomfortable," can go a long way.

2. Establishing Trust

Trust is foundational to any feedback exchange. If someone trusts you, they are more likely to believe that your feedback comes from a place of genuine care and support. Trust, according to **Stephen M.R. Covey**, author of *The Speed of Trust*, is built through consistent actions, transparency, and integrity.

How to Build Trust:

- **Consistency**: Be consistent in your behaviour and communication. If people know what to expect from you, they'll feel more secure.

- **Follow Through**: If you promise to support someone's development after giving feedback, ensure you do so. Empty promises can damage trust.

- **Be Honest but Kind**: Being honest doesn't mean being harsh. Deliver feedback truthfully but considerately.

3. Choosing the Right Setting

The physical environment where feedback is given can also influence how well it is received. For instance, giving feedback in a private, quiet space can make the recipient feel more comfortable compared to doing it in a public or high-stress area.

- **Private Spaces**: Feedback, especially negative feedback, should be delivered privately to respect the recipient's dignity.
- **Minimize Distractions**: Make sure the space is free from noise, interruptions, or other distractions that could detract from the conversation.
- **Body Language Matters**: Sit at eye level with the recipient, maintain open body language, and avoid putting barriers, such as a desk, between you.

Case Study: A major company, **IBM**, revamped its feedback culture by redesigning office spaces to include more private feedback rooms. This small change led to a significant increase in employee satisfaction with feedback conversations, as reported in their internal HR data.

Techniques to Create a Feedback-Friendly Culture

1. Normalize Feedback as a Regular Practice

Instead of only giving feedback during formal reviews or when something goes wrong, normalize it as part of everyday interactions. The more regular feedback becomes, the less intimidating it feels.

Tip: Schedule routine "feedback check-ins" where both parties can exchange thoughts in a low-pressure context. These meetings can be brief, but their regularity creates an open-door policy for feedback.

2. Use "Feedforward" Techniques

Introduced by **Marshall Goldsmith**, the concept of "feedforward" involves focusing on future behaviour rather than dwelling on past mistakes. Instead of only critiquing what went wrong, provide suggestions for improvement moving forward.

- *Example*: Instead of saying, "You didn't perform well in that meeting," try, "Next time, let's work on how to engage the audience more effectively."

This forward-looking approach is often perceived as more constructive and motivating.

3. Encourage Two-Way Feedback

For feedback to be most effective, it should be a dialogue, not a monologue. Invite the recipient to share their perspective and thoughts on the feedback. This not only makes the conversation more collaborative but also demonstrates that you value their input.

- **Ask Open-Ended Questions**: "What are your thoughts on this?" or "How do you feel about the suggestions I've shared?"
- **Be Willing to Listen**: Sometimes, feedback recipients may have valuable insights that can inform how feedback is delivered in the future.

Example Scenario: Transforming a Difficult Feedback Environment

Imagine a scenario in a school setting where teachers feel demoralized due to the administration's harsh and inconsistent feedback practices. The school principal, realizing the negative impact, decides to change the approach:

1. **Psychological Safety Initiatives**: The principal organizes monthly "listening sessions" where teachers can voice concerns without fear of reprisal.
2. **Trust-Building Exercises**: Administrators begin attending classes, not to evaluate but to understand teachers' challenges. Over time, teachers begin to trust that feedback is given in the spirit of collaboration, not judgment.
3. **Improved Physical Spaces**: Feedback sessions are moved to inviting, comfortable rooms instead of the principal's intimidating office. This shift contributes to more open and productive discussions.

Outcome: Over a year, teacher satisfaction scores rise significantly, and the school reports an increase in student engagement, linked to improved teacher morale and performance.

Creating a supportive environment for feedback conversations requires intentionality. By fostering psychological safety, building trust, choosing the right settings, and employing thoughtful feedback practices, you pave the way for meaningful and effective communication. The next chapter will explore how to structure your feedback using specific frameworks that ensure clarity and impact.

Chapter 5

The Art of Choosing Your Words

The words you use can either uplift and inspire or hurt and alienate.

Words are powerful. When it comes to giving feedback, the language you use can greatly impact how the recipient perceives and responds to your message. Using careful, thoughtful, and constructive language can make feedback more palatable, even when it addresses difficult or sensitive topics. This chapter will guide you through strategies for choosing your words with care and intention, ensuring that your message is clear, empathetic, and impactful.

Why Word Choice Matters

Feedback is not just about content but also about how it is communicated. According to communication scholars like **Deborah Tannen**, the nuances of language—such as tone, word choice, and phrasing—affect how messages are received. Tannen's work on conversational style reveals that subtle differences in language can influence perceptions and relationships. For example, phrases that sound accusatory or critical can make the recipient defensive, while those framed positively can encourage collaboration.

A study in **Organizational Behaviour and Human Decision Processes** found that feedback phrased in a way that emphasizes growth and learning (a "growth-oriented language") motivates individuals more effectively than feedback that focuses on failure or inadequacy. Words have the power to shape someone's mindset and willingness to engage in improvement.

Strategies for Effective Language in Feedback

1. Use "I" Statements Instead of "You" Statements

"I" statements express how the speaker feels or perceives a situation without making the recipient feel blamed. This approach softens the message and reduces the chances of a defensive reaction.

- *Less Effective*: "You never listen during team meetings."
- *More Effective*: "I've noticed that I sometimes have to repeat myself in team meetings, and I feel it might be because we could improve our listening skills as a group."

Why It Works: "I" statements focus on your perspective rather than placing blame. This subtle shift helps maintain a collaborative and respectful tone.

Communication Insight: The technique of using "I" statements has been widely endorsed in conflict resolution research, such as the work of **Marshall Rosenberg**, who developed *Nonviolent Communication* as a framework for compassionate and effective dialogue.

2. Be Specific and Descriptive

Generalizations and vague language make feedback less actionable. Specific language provides clarity and gives the recipient concrete information they can work with.

- *Vague Feedback*: "You need to be more professional."
- *Specific Feedback*: "I noticed during yesterday's client presentation that we lost track of time and didn't finish the Q&A. Keeping track of the schedule will help us maintain professionalism in future meetings."

Case Study: In a study at **Microsoft**, managers who shifted from general comments to detailed, behaviour-based feedback reported higher employee satisfaction and more significant performance improvements. The change was most effective when feedback included a clear example and a suggested path forward.

3. Use Neutral and Non-Loaded Language

Avoid emotionally charged words that can escalate tensions. Terms like "lazy," "incompetent," or "disastrous" come across as judgmental and can alienate the recipient. Instead, use neutral descriptors that focus on observable behaviour.

- *Emotionally Charged*: "Your report was a complete disaster."
- *Neutral*: "The report had several areas for improvement, such as the data analysis section, which lacked supporting evidence."

Neuroscience Insight: Research on emotional regulation and language, such as the work of **Dr. Matthew Lieberman** at UCLA, shows that loaded language activates the brain's threat response. This makes it harder for the recipient to process constructive feedback and more likely for them to respond emotionally.

4. Frame Feedback in a Growth Mindset

Psychologist **Carol Dweck**'s work on mindset highlights that framing challenges as opportunities for growth encourages people to embrace feedback and learn from it. Instead of labelling behaviour as inherently bad or wrong, suggest ways it can be improved.

- *Fixed Mindset*: "You're not good at public speaking."
- *Growth Mindset*: "You've made progress in your public speaking skills, and I think focusing on eye contact and engaging your audience more will help you continue to improve."

Tip: Use language that emphasizes learning, such as "let's work on this together" or "this is an opportunity to grow."

The Power of Positive Language

Positive language does not mean avoiding difficult topics; rather, it focuses on constructive suggestions and reinforces the potential for change. Words that emphasize strengths while acknowledging areas for improvement are more motivating and less likely to be perceived as criticism.

5. Use "And" Instead of "But"

The word "but" can negate everything that precedes it, making positive statements sound insincere. Replacing "but" with "and" helps to balance the feedback without diminishing the positive aspects.

- *Less Effective*: "You did a great job on the project, but your time management needs work."
- *More Effective*: "You did a great job on the project, and working on time management could make your next project even better."

Linguistic Research: A study in the *Journal of Applied Psychology* showed that recipients of feedback framed with "and" instead of "but" rated the feedback as more constructive and encouraging.

6. Ask Questions to Invite Engagement

Instead of making statements that could feel authoritarian, use questions to engage the recipient in a dialogue. Questions create a sense of shared responsibility and open up opportunities for problem-solving.

- *Directive Statement*: "You need to handle clients better."
- *Engaging Question*: "What strategies do you think we could use to improve our interactions with clients?"

Why It Works: Asking questions fosters collaboration and shows respect for the recipient's input. According to **research from the Centre for Creative Leadership**, feedback that involves dialogue rather than monologue is more likely to result in positive behavioural change.

Avoiding Common Pitfalls in Language

1. Avoid Absolutes (e.g., "Always," "Never")

Absolutes can make the recipient feel unfairly judged, especially if there are exceptions. Instead, use phrases that leave room for nuance.

- *Absolute Statement*: "You never pay attention to details."
- *Alternative*: "I've noticed instances where some details were overlooked, such as in last week's report."

2. Avoid Making It Personal

Feedback should be about behaviour or outcomes, not about the person's character. Personal judgments damage relationships and make feedback less effective.

- *Personal Critique*: "You're careless and irresponsible."
- *Behavioural Feedback*: "The documents you submitted had several errors, which we should work on reducing."

Leadership Insight: Effective leaders, according to a study by **Brene Brown** on vulnerability and courage, avoid shaming language. They focus on fostering accountability without attacking someone's character.

Practical Example: A Workplace Scenario

Imagine a project manager named Alex who needs to give feedback to a team member, Jordan, who often submits reports late. Here's how Alex can apply these strategies:

1. **"I" Statement**: "I've noticed that I often receive the reports a day after the deadline, and it impacts our ability to move forward on time."
2. **Specific Example**: "For example, the quarterly financial report last week was delayed, which affected our planning session."
3. **Neutral Language**: "This is an area we could improve together."

4. **Growth-Oriented Frame**: "I know you're capable of meeting these deadlines, and I'd like to explore how I can support you better to make that happen."

Outcome: Jordan feels respected and understands the impact of their behaviour without feeling personally attacked. The conversation becomes an opportunity for problem-solving rather than conflict.

Choosing your words carefully is not about sugarcoating the truth; it's about delivering feedback in a way that inspires change, fosters respect, and promotes a constructive dialogue. Words are powerful tools and using them wisely can transform difficult conversations into moments of connection and growth. The next chapter will explore the art of listening actively and empathetically, an essential skill for any successful feedback exchange.

Chapter 6

The Role of Active Listening

Effective feedback is as much about listening as it is about speaking.

Giving feedback is an essential skill, but equally important is the ability to listen actively and empathetically. When you genuinely listen, you show respect for the recipient's perspective, encourage open dialogue, and gain insights that can enhance your understanding of the situation. Active listening transforms feedback conversations from one-sided critiques into collaborative problem-solving opportunities.

Why Active Listening Is Crucial in Feedback

Active listening goes beyond hearing words; it involves understanding the speaker's intent, emotions, and concerns. **Carl Rogers**, a pioneer in the field of humanistic psychology, emphasized that active listening builds trust and empathy, which are crucial in any meaningful conversation. He argued that people are more likely to be open and receptive when they feel heard and understood.

A study published in the *International Journal of Listening* demonstrated that managers who practiced active listening had better outcomes in feedback conversations. Employees reported feeling more valued and were more likely to act on the feedback received. The study also revealed that active listening leads to increased job satisfaction and a stronger sense of belonging in the workplace.

Components of Active Listening

1. Give Your Full Attention

Active listening starts with being fully present. This means putting away distractions, making eye contact, and showing through your body language that you are engaged.

- **Body Language**: Maintain eye contact, nod occasionally to show understanding, and use open gestures. Avoid crossing your arms or looking at your phone, as these behaviours can signal disinterest.
- **Eliminate Distractions**: Turn off notifications on your devices, and choose a quiet location for the conversation.

Example: A manager who stops typing on their computer and turns to face the employee during a feedback session demonstrates active listening. This simple act can make a significant difference in how the conversation unfolds.

2. Reflect and Paraphrase

Reflecting or paraphrasing what the other person says shows that you are truly listening and understanding their message. This technique also gives the speaker a chance to clarify or expand on their thoughts.

- **Paraphrasing**: "So, what I'm hearing is that you felt overwhelmed by the project deadline and found it hard to prioritize. Is that correct?"
- **Reflecting Emotion**: "It sounds like this situation was really frustrating for you."

Why It Works: Reflecting not only confirms that you are paying attention but also validates the speaker's emotions. According to **Dr. John Gottman**, a relationship researcher, validation is a key component of successful communication. People feel more at ease when they know their emotions and perspectives are acknowledged.

3. Ask Open-Ended Questions

Instead of asking questions that can be answered with a simple "yes" or "no," use open-ended questions to encourage deeper discussion. This technique invites the recipient to share their thoughts and feelings.

- **Examples of Open-Ended Questions**:
    - "Can you walk me through what happened from your perspective?"
    - "What do you think would be a helpful way to address this challenge?"
    - "How do you feel about the feedback I've given?"

Benefit: Open-ended questions foster a two-way dialogue, making the feedback conversation more engaging and productive. **Harvard Business Review** has highlighted that leaders who ask thoughtful questions during feedback discussions are more successful in facilitating meaningful change.

4. Listen to Understand, Not to Respond

Many people listen with the intent to reply, rather than to understand. Active listening requires you to focus on comprehending the speaker's message fully before preparing your response.

- **Mindset Shift**: Remind yourself that the goal is to understand the other person's perspective, not to defend your own or immediately offer solutions.
- **Pause Before Responding**: After the person finishes speaking, take a moment to process their words before replying. This pause shows that you value their input and are thoughtfully considering what they've said.

Communication Insight: **Stephen Covey**, in his book *The 7 Habits of Highly Effective People*, emphasizes the importance of understanding before being understood. Covey argues that empathetic listening builds the foundation for mutual respect and understanding, crucial for effective communication.

Techniques for Mastering Active Listening

1. Practice Mindful Listening

Mindful listening involves being fully present and aware of your surroundings, thoughts, and feelings while listening. It requires conscious effort to set aside distractions and judgments.

- **Mindfulness Exercise**: Before a feedback session, take a few deep breaths to centre yourself. This practice can help you remain calm and focused throughout the conversation.
- **Stay Aware of Biases**: Everyone has unconscious biases that can affect how they interpret information. Being mindful helps you recognize and set aside these biases.

Scientific Insight: **Mindfulness training**, as explored by researchers like **Dr. Jon Kabat-Zinn**, has been shown to improve listening skills and empathy. It can enhance your ability to engage in meaningful conversations and respond with greater clarity and understanding.

2. Show Empathy

Empathy is the ability to understand and share the feelings of another person. In feedback conversations, showing empathy means being sensitive to how the recipient might be feeling and responding in a way that acknowledges those emotions.

- **Empathetic Statements**: "I understand that this feedback might be difficult to hear, and I appreciate your willingness to discuss it."
- **Nonverbal Cues**: Sometimes, a compassionate nod or a gentle tone of voice can convey empathy more effectively than words.

Emotional Intelligence: Psychologist **Daniel Goleman** emphasizes that empathy is a key component of emotional intelligence, which is essential for effective leadership and communication. People are more likely to respond positively to feedback when they feel understood on an emotional level.

Active Listening in Practice: A Real-World Example

Scenario: A team leader, Maria, needs to give feedback to an employee, Sam, who has been missing deadlines. Instead of starting with a critique, Maria asks, "Can you tell me what's been going on with your workload lately?" Sam explains that he's been struggling with a personal issue that has affected his focus.

- **Maria's Active Listening**: She reflects, "It sounds like you've been going through a tough time, and that's been impacting your work. I appreciate you sharing that with me."
- **Outcome**: Because Maria listened actively, she understands the root cause of the issue. They discuss potential solutions, like adjusting deadlines temporarily or offering additional support. Sam feels valued and understood, making him more open to suggestions for improvement.

Impact: By practicing active listening, Maria turns a potentially uncomfortable feedback session into a collaborative problem-solving conversation. This not only improves their working relationship but also leads to a more supportive work environment.

Overcoming Common Barriers to Active Listening

1. Preconceptions and Judgments

It's easy to form judgments before hearing the full story. To overcome this, remind yourself that your goal is to understand, not to judge.

- **Tip**: If you notice yourself making assumptions, pause and refocus on the speaker's words. Practice withholding judgment until you have all the information.

2. Emotional Triggers

Sometimes, the feedback conversation can bring up strong emotions, especially if you disagree with what the other person is saying. In such cases, practice emotional regulation.

- **Strategy**: Take a deep breath and remind yourself to stay calm. If necessary, ask for a moment to collect your thoughts.

Example: If a colleague says something you perceive as unfair, resist the urge to interrupt or defend yourself. Listen to their full perspective before responding thoughtfully.

Active listening is a skill that can transform feedback conversations from confrontational to constructive. By being present, reflecting, asking open-ended questions, and showing empathy, you create a space where both parties feel respected and understood. As we move into the next chapter, we'll discuss strategies for handling difficult emotions during feedback, both your own and the recipient's, to ensure that even the most challenging conversations remain productive and respectful.

Chapter 7

Managing Difficult Emotions

Emotion is a powerful force in any interaction, but managing it effectively can turn a difficult conversation into a constructive one.

Giving and receiving feedback often stirs up emotions, ranging from anxiety and frustration to vulnerability and defensiveness. While it's natural to experience emotional reactions, understanding and managing them is key to ensuring feedback conversations remain productive. This chapter explores strategies to handle difficult emotions—for both the feedback giver and receiver—to foster a supportive and growth-oriented dialogue.

Understanding the Emotional Dynamics of Feedback

Feedback conversations are inherently emotional because they often involve our sense of identity, competence, and self-worth. **Sheila Heen** and **Douglas Stone**, authors of *Thanks for the Feedback*, argue that feedback triggers emotional responses that can make or break the conversation. These responses are typically rooted in three triggers:

1. **Truth Triggers**: When feedback feels inaccurate or unfair.

2. **Relationship Triggers**: When the source of the feedback affects how it is received (e.g., feedback from a colleague versus a superior).

3. **Identity Triggers**: When feedback challenges our sense of who we are, making us feel vulnerable or insecure.

Heen and Stone emphasize that awareness of these triggers can help us manage our emotional reactions more effectively.

Example: If someone criticizes your communication skills, you might feel defensive because it challenges your self-image as a strong communicator. Recognizing this identity trigger can help you process the feedback without letting emotions take over.

Strategies for Managing Your Own Emotions

1. Practice Emotional Awareness

Understanding your emotional triggers can help you anticipate and manage your reactions during feedback conversations. Emotional awareness is about recognizing what you feel and why.

- **Self-Reflection**: Before a feedback conversation, reflect on how you feel. Are you anxious, frustrated, or defensive? Understanding your emotional state can help you stay composed.

- **Name Your Emotions**: Psychologists like **Dr. Dan Siegel** recommend "naming your emotions to tame them." Simply acknowledging that you feel anxious or angry can help you manage those emotions better.

Example: Before providing feedback, take a moment to note any anxiety or stress you're feeling. This awareness can help you approach the conversation calmly.

2. Use Grounding Techniques

Grounding techniques can help you manage intense emotions in the moment. These strategies bring your focus back to the present and reduce emotional overwhelm.

- **Deep Breathing**: Take slow, deep breaths to calm your nervous system. Breathing deeply signals to your brain that it's safe to relax, reducing feelings of anxiety.

- **5-4-3-2-1 Technique**: Focus on five things you can see, four things you can touch, three things you can hear, two things you can smell, and one thing you can taste. This exercise helps bring your attention back to the present.

Neuroscience Insight: Studies have shown that deep breathing can lower cortisol levels, the hormone associated with stress. The **American Institute of Stress** recommends deep breathing as a simple yet effective way to manage emotional intensity.

3. Prepare a Script

If you're worried about getting emotional, consider preparing a script or outline of what you want to say. Having a plan can reduce anxiety and help you communicate your points more clearly.

- **Use Empathetic Language**: Prepare phrases that express understanding and compassion, such as "I know this might be difficult to hear" or "I appreciate your openness to this conversation."

Benefit: Scripts can serve as a safety net, allowing you to stay on track even if emotions run high.

Helping the Recipient Manage Their Emotions

1. Create a Safe Environment

A supportive and non-judgmental atmosphere encourages the recipient to process feedback constructively. Safety means feeling respected, valued, and free from judgment.

- **Private Setting**: Choose a private space for the conversation to minimize embarrassment or pressure.
- **Open Body Language**: Sit or stand in a non-confrontational way. Avoid crossing your arms, which can appear defensive or closed off.

Example: If you're providing feedback about performance issues, ensure that the recipient feels respected and understood by expressing empathy and maintaining an open posture.

2. Use Empathy to Acknowledge Emotions

Acknowledge the recipient's emotions, even if you don't agree with their reaction. Validating their feelings doesn't mean you are conceding the point; it simply shows you understand their perspective.

- **Empathetic Statements**: "I can see that this feedback is upsetting, and I understand why you feel that way."
- **Active Listening**: Allow the recipient to express their emotions without interrupting. Sometimes, people just need to vent before they can engage productively.

Empathy Research: According to **Dr. Brené Brown**, empathy is the antidote to shame and defensiveness. When people feel seen and heard, they are more likely to be open to feedback.

3. Encourage a Growth Mindset

Remind the recipient that feedback is a tool for growth, not a judgment of their worth. Emphasizing a growth mindset can help shift the focus from defensiveness to learning.

- **Growth-Oriented Language**: "This feedback is an opportunity for us to work on something together and get even better."
- **Acknowledge Effort**: If the recipient has been working hard, recognize that effort before diving into areas for improvement.

Psychology Insight: **Carol Dweck**'s research on growth mindset shows that people who view challenges as opportunities to learn are more resilient and open to constructive feedback.

Tools for Emotional Regulation During Feedback

1. Use "Emotion Coaches" or Mediators

In high-stakes or emotionally charged situations, consider bringing in a neutral third party to mediate the conversation. This could be an HR representative, or a trusted colleague trained in conflict resolution, without a vested interest in a particular outcome.

Benefit: Emotion coaches can help de-escalate tension and ensure that both parties feel heard and respected.

2. Take Breaks if Necessary

If emotions run too high and the conversation becomes unproductive, it's okay to suggest a short break. Returning to the discussion after cooling off can lead to a more constructive outcome.

- **Example**: "I think we're both feeling a bit overwhelmed right now. Would you be open to taking a five-minute break and coming back to this?"

Communication Insight: The **Journal of Applied Psychology** reports that taking breaks during heated conversations can significantly reduce stress and improve communication outcomes.

Real-World Scenarios: Managing Emotions Effectively

Scenario 1: Giving Feedback to a Defensive Colleague Imagine you need to give feedback to a colleague, Chris, who tends to get defensive. You start the conversation by acknowledging their strengths: "Chris, I really value the creativity you bring to our team." Then, you address the feedback gently: "I've noticed that some deadlines have been missed recently, and I'd like to understand how we can address this together." When Chris becomes defensive, you respond with empathy: "I hear that you're feeling overwhelmed. Let's talk about how we can make this more manageable."

Outcome: By validating Chris's emotions and inviting collaboration, the conversation remains constructive.

DELIVERING NEGATIVE FEEDBACK

Scenario 2: Receiving Critical Feedback. You're on the receiving end of critical feedback from your manager, who points out mistakes in a recent project. Instead of reacting defensively, you use grounding techniques, like taking a few deep breaths. You listen actively and repeat back what you heard to ensure you understand: "So, you're saying the analysis I presented lacked detail, and you'd like to see more thorough research next time." You then ask for suggestions on how to improve: "What resources or strategies would you recommend to enhance the analysis?"

Outcome: By managing your emotions and seeking solutions, you demonstrate maturity and a commitment to growth.

Emotional regulation is a critical skill for navigating feedback conversations with grace and effectiveness. By understanding and managing your own emotions and creating a safe space for others to express theirs, you can transform even the most challenging feedback into a meaningful exchange. In the next chapter, we'll explore how to structure feedback conversations to maximize clarity and impact, ensuring that your message is well-received and actionable.

Chapter 8

Structuring Feedback: Conversations for Maximum Impact

The success of any feedback conversation often lies in how it is structured.

Whether you're delivering positive feedback, constructive criticism, or a mix of both, the way you organize your message has a profound effect on how it is received. A well-structured feedback conversation is clear, respectful, and actionable. In this chapter, we'll explore effective frameworks, best practices, and examples that ensure your feedback lands with impact and fosters genuine improvement.

Why Structure Matters in Feedback

According to communication experts **Douglas Stone** and **Sheila Heen**, structuring feedback appropriately helps minimize misunderstandings and emotional resistance. The **Centre for Creative Leadership** also emphasizes that disorganized or vague feedback often leads to confusion, defensiveness, and demotivation. On the other hand, clear and structured conversations create a shared understanding of goals and expectations.

Example: Compare saying, "You need to be more organized," with a structured approach: "I've noticed that some of your project deadlines have been missed. Let's discuss how we can improve organization and meet future timelines." The latter sets a collaborative tone and focuses on specific behaviours.

Frameworks for Structuring Effective Feedback

1. The "SBI Model" (Situation-Behaviour-Impact)

The SBI Model, developed by the **Centre for Creative Leadership**, is a straightforward approach for giving clear and specific feedback. It helps focus on observable behaviours rather than making generalized or subjective statements.

- **Situation**: Describe the context of the behaviour.
- **Behaviour**: Explain exactly what the person did.
- **Impact**: Share the effect of the behaviour on you, the team, or the organization.

Example:

- **Situation**: "In yesterday's team meeting…"
- **Behaviour**: "…when you interrupted John several times while he was presenting…"
- **Impact**: "…it disrupted the flow of the discussion and made it difficult for others to share their thoughts."

Benefit: The SBI Model minimizes ambiguity and focuses on behaviours rather than personal traits, making the feedback feel less like a personal attack and more like a constructive observation.

2. The "DESC Model" (Describe, Express, Specify, Consequences)

The DESC Model, recommended in assertiveness training, is designed to provide feedback assertively without being aggressive or passive.

- **Describe**: Clearly describe the behaviour you observed.
- **Express**: Express your feelings or concerns about the behaviour.
- **Specify**: Specify what you would like to see happen differently in the future.
- **Consequences**: Explain the positive outcomes that will result from the change.

Example:

- **Describe**: "I've noticed that your reports are often submitted late…"
- **Express**: "…which makes it challenging for the rest of the team to stay on schedule."
- **Specify**: "Could you prioritize submitting reports on time in the future?"
- **Consequences**: "If reports are submitted on time, the entire team will be able to work more efficiently."

Impact: The DESC Model ensures that feedback is assertive yet respectful, making the recipient more receptive to change.

3. The "Feedforward" Approach

Proposed by **Marshall Goldsmith**, the feedforward method focuses on future improvements rather than past mistakes. Instead of dwelling on what went wrong, this approach emphasizes positive steps for growth.

- **How It Works**: Instead of saying, "You didn't communicate well in that meeting," you might say, "Next time, consider summarizing your key points at the beginning to keep the audience engaged."
- **Benefit**: Feedforward reduces defensiveness and keeps the conversation solution-focused. Research by **Goldsmith** suggests that this forward-looking approach can be more motivating and less emotionally charged.

Real-World Example: In a performance review, instead of criticizing an employee for past inefficiencies, a manager could discuss how adopting new time-management techniques could boost productivity moving forward.

Preparing for the Feedback Conversation

1. Clarify Your Objectives

Before giving feedback, be clear about what you want to achieve. Are you hoping to improve performance, address a behavioural issue, or encourage a particular action? Having a clear goal in mind will help you structure your message effectively.

- **Tip**: Write down your key points and desired outcomes. Preparation can help you stay focused and concise.

2. Choose the Right Timing and Setting

The timing and environment can significantly influence how feedback is received.

- **Timing**: Give feedback soon after the behaviour occurs, while the details are fresh. However, avoid giving feedback when emotions are high, either for you or the recipient.
- **Setting**: Choose a private and neutral space where the recipient feels comfortable. Public feedback can feel humiliating, even if your intentions are good.

Example: If an employee mishandles a client interaction, address it promptly but privately, such as scheduling a one-on-one meeting later that day.

Techniques to Keep the Conversation Productive

1. Use the "Sandwich" Method (with Caution)

The sandwich method involves delivering constructive feedback between two positive comments. While this technique can soften the blow, it has its limitations.

- **Example**: "I appreciate your creativity in the project (positive). However, the presentation had several factual inaccuracies (constructive feedback). I know you have the skills to double-check details, and I'm confident in your abilities (positive)."
- **Caution**: Be careful not to dilute the constructive feedback too much, as this can make it seem insincere or confusing. Some experts, like **Dr. Bob Sutton**, argue that the sandwich method can feel disingenuous if overused.

2. Use "I" Statements to Reduce Defensiveness

Using "I" statements instead of "you" statements can make feedback less accusatory.

- **Example**: Instead of saying, "You never listen to the team's ideas," try, "I feel that team ideas are sometimes overlooked, and I'd love to see more open discussions."

Communication Insight: Research from the **Journal of Communication** highlights that "I" statements promote a sense of collaboration and reduce defensiveness.

3. Be Specific and Actionable

Vague feedback is rarely helpful. Be as specific as possible and suggest concrete actions.

- **Poor Feedback**: "Your work needs to be better."
- **Better Feedback**: "Your last report had several errors. In the future, could you review your work more thoroughly or use a checklist to ensure accuracy?"

Benefit: Actionable feedback provides a clear path forward, increasing the likelihood of positive change.

Handling Emotional Reactions to Structured Feedback

Even when feedback is well-structured, emotions can run high. Here's how to manage emotional responses effectively:

1. Pause and Listen

If the recipient becomes defensive or upset, pause and give them a chance to speak. Active listening, as discussed in the previous chapter, shows that you respect their feelings.

2. Reiterate Your Intentions

Sometimes, emotions flare up because the recipient misinterprets your intentions. Reaffirm that your goal is to help them grow and succeed.

- **Example**: "I understand this is hard to hear. Please know that I'm sharing this feedback because I want to see you succeed."

Structuring Feedback for Different Personalities

Feedback isn't one-size-fits-all. People have different communication styles, and understanding these differences can help you tailor your approach.

1. Analytical Personalities

People who are data-driven and detail-oriented may appreciate feedback that includes specific examples and metrics.

- **Example**: "You missed two deadlines last month, which affected the project timeline. Let's discuss strategies to prevent this in the future."

2. Emotional Personalities

Those who are more emotionally sensitive may benefit from a gentler approach that emphasizes empathy and support.

- **Example**: "I know you've been working hard, and I appreciate that. Let's talk about how we can improve your time management to reduce stress."

Psychology Insight: According to **Dr. David Keirsey**, understanding personality types can improve communication and make feedback more effective.

Structuring feedback conversations thoughtfully can make the difference between resistance and receptiveness. By using frameworks like the SBI Model, the DESC Model, and the feedforward approach, you ensure your feedback is clear, respectful, and geared toward positive outcomes. In the next chapter, we'll explore how to handle feedback situations that escalate into conflicts, equipping you with strategies to navigate difficult conversations with confidence and poise.

Chapter 9

Coaching Others: Turn Negative Feedback into Actionable Improvement

As the giver of feedback, your role is not only to deliver criticism but also to guide the recipient toward using that feedback for meaningful change.

Delivering negative feedback can feel like a delicate task. However, as a coach or leader, your responsibility doesn't end with just pointing out areas of improvement. You also play a pivotal role in helping the recipient understand, internalize, and act on the feedback constructively. In this chapter, we'll explore how to not only deliver effective feedback but also empower the recipient to use it as a tool for growth and improvement.

The Role of a Feedback Coach

Feedback is most effective when it's treated as a collaborative process rather than a one-way transmission of criticism. You're not just giving feedback—you're coaching the recipient on how to interpret, reflect, and take actionable steps from it. As a feedback giver, your goal is to create a supportive environment where the recipient feels empowered to take ownership of their development.

Research Insight: Studies by the **Centre for Creative Leadership** highlight that feedback is more likely to lead to improvement when it is part of an ongoing dialogue, rather than a single, isolated conversation. Coaches or managers who offer guidance on how to act on feedback help recipients make lasting changes.

DELIVERING NEGATIVE FEEDBACK

1. Setting the Stage for Constructive Feedback

Creating an environment where feedback is welcomed and seen as an opportunity for growth is essential. Begin by setting the right tone for the conversation, making it clear that your intention is to help the recipient improve and develop.

Key Tips for Setting the Stage:

- **Ensure Emotional Readiness**: Before delivering negative feedback, make sure the person is in the right emotional space to receive it. For example, ask if they're open to feedback at the moment. This allows the recipient to mentally prepare and lowers defensiveness.

- **Create a Safe, Private Space**: Ensure the conversation takes place in a private, respectful setting, where the recipient feels comfortable and not publicly criticized.

- **Frame the Feedback as a Positive Opportunity**: Begin the conversation by emphasizing that feedback is an essential part of growth and improvement. This helps the recipient understand that the goal is to develop their skills and not to point out flaws.

Example: "I'd like to talk about an area where I think we can make some improvements. My goal is to help you grow, and I believe this feedback will be valuable in achieving that."

2. Guiding Reflection: Helping the Recipient Understand the Feedback

Once you've delivered the feedback, it's crucial to guide the recipient through a reflective process. This helps them understand both the content and the underlying message behind the feedback, which enables them to use it for growth.

Coaching Tips for Reflection:

- **Ask Open-Ended Questions**: Encourage the recipient to reflect on the feedback by asking questions like, "What do you think went wrong in this situation?" or "How do you think you could approach this differently next time?" These questions help them take ownership of the feedback and identify areas for improvement themselves.

- **Encourage Self-Assessment**: Allow the recipient to assess their own performance before you offer further insights. Self-awareness is a critical aspect of growth. For example, "How do you think your approach could have been more effective in this case?"

- **Focus on Specifics**: It's essential to ensure that feedback is specific. If the feedback is vague, encourage the recipient to ask for examples or clarifications. "Can you give me an example of when you felt that my response was unclear or ineffective?"

Example: After offering feedback about missed deadlines, you might ask, "What do you think caused the delays in your last project? What might you try differently to prevent that in the future?"

3. Moving from Reflection to Action: Helping the Recipient Create a Plan

Once the recipient has had time to reflect on the feedback, your role as a coach is to help them turn that reflection into concrete, actionable steps for improvement. The most powerful feedback is feedback that is followed by action.

Coaching Tips for Creating Action Plans:

- **Set SMART Goals**: Help the recipient develop specific, measurable, achievable, relevant, and time-bound goals to address the areas of feedback. For example, if the feedback is about improving time management, work together to set a goal like: "By the end of this month, I will implement a daily planner to track all of my tasks and meet at least 90% of my deadlines."

- **Encourage Small Steps**: Breaking down the improvement plan into manageable steps increases the likelihood of success. Instead of trying to change everything at once, identify one or two key areas for improvement and focus on those.

- **Develop New Habits**: Feedback is most effective when it encourages lasting changes. Work with the recipient to develop new habits and practices that will address the feedback and lead to sustained improvement.

Example: If the feedback involves better communication, help them create a plan to:

- Schedule regular check-ins with team members.
- Practice active listening by summarizing others' points before responding.

4. Providing Support: Reinforcing Positive Changes

As a coach, your role doesn't end with delivering feedback and helping the recipient create a plan. Regular follow-up is essential for ensuring that feedback leads to lasting improvement. Reinforcing positive changes helps the recipient stay motivated and on track.

Coaching Tips for Providing Ongoing Support:

- **Regular Check-Ins**: Schedule follow-up conversations to monitor progress. In these check-ins, ask how they're implementing the feedback, and offer support in overcoming any challenges they may be facing.
- **Celebrate Small Wins**: Acknowledge the effort they're putting into implementing the feedback, even if the improvement is gradual. Celebrating small successes builds confidence and keeps them motivated.
- **Encourage Continuous Improvement**: Feedback is a process, not a one-time event. Encourage the recipient to view feedback as an ongoing part of their development. "We're always learning and improving. Let's revisit this in a month and see how things have progressed."

Example: "You did a great job managing your deadlines last month, but we'll continue to refine your approach. Let's keep working on it, and I'm here to help."

5. Addressing Resistance: Overcoming Obstacles to Feedback Acceptance

It's not uncommon for people to resist feedback, particularly negative feedback. As a coach, part of your job is to help the recipient work through that resistance.

Coaching Tips for Overcoming Resistance:

- **Be Empathetic**: Understand that receiving negative feedback can trigger emotions like embarrassment or defensiveness. Acknowledge their feelings and reassure them that the feedback is meant to be constructive, not personal.

- **Normalize the Experience**: Help the recipient understand that everyone has areas for growth. When possible, share examples of your own experiences with receiving feedback to create a sense of solidarity.

- **Foster Trust**: The more trust you build, the more likely the recipient is to accept feedback. Be consistent, supportive, and fair in your approach to ensure that they see the feedback as an opportunity for development rather than a criticism.

Research Insight: According to **Dr. David Rock's SCARF model**, when individuals feel respected and valued, they are more open to feedback. Building trust and reducing emotional threats encourages a more positive reception of criticism.

6. Tailoring Your Approach: Adapting Feedback to Individual Needs

Not all recipients of feedback are the same, so it's important to adapt your coaching approach based on their individual needs and personalities. Some people respond well to detailed, structured feedback, while others may need more encouragement and support.

Key Adaptations:

- **For Analytical Thinkers**: Focus on data and examples. They may appreciate feedback that is clear, objective, and backed by evidence.

- **For Emotional Responders**: Use a more empathetic, supportive approach. Acknowledge their feelings and create a safe space for them to discuss the feedback without fear of judgment.

- **For Independent Learners**: Provide autonomy in the feedback process. Encourage them to develop their own solutions but offer guidance when needed.

Example: If you're coaching an employee who is more analytical, you might provide specific data points and case studies. For someone more emotional, you might offer reassurance and validation before diving into the specifics.

By adopting a coaching mindset and guiding your recipient through the feedback process, you can help them turn negative feedback into actionable improvement. Your role is not just to deliver criticism, but to empower the recipient to reflect, plan, and take steps toward growth. In the next chapter, we will explore how to handle more complex feedback situations, where multiple stakeholders or conflicting feedback may be involved.

BEN SORENSEN

Chapter 10

Navigating Difficult Feedback: How to Handle Contradictory or Conflicting Feedback

As a feedback giver, one of the most complex challenges you may face is delivering feedback that conflicts with feedback from others, or addressing contradictory feedback a recipient has received. It's essential to handle these situations delicately to ensure that feedback remains valuable and actionable.

While negative feedback is often straightforward, situations where contradictory or conflicting feedback arises can leave both the giver and the recipient feeling confused or frustrated. When a person receives feedback from different sources that doesn't align, it can be difficult for them to know which direction to take. As a feedback giver, it's your responsibility to guide them through this complexity, helping them to understand the different perspectives and decide on the best course of action for their development.

1. Understanding the Nature of Conflicting Feedback

Conflicting feedback typically arises in workplaces, team environments, or coaching situations where multiple stakeholders provide input on the same performance or behaviour. This feedback may come from colleagues, supervisors, mentors, or peers, and it can range from differing views on how well someone is performing to contradictory suggestions on how to improve.

The Sources of Conflicting Feedback:
- **Different Perspectives**: People in different roles (e.g., managers, peers, or clients) may have different expectations, priorities, and experiences. What one person sees as a minor issue, another might view as a significant problem.

- **Communication Gaps**: Miscommunication or incomplete information can result in feedback that lacks clarity or consistency. Sometimes, feedback is based on incomplete observations or assumptions.
- **Cultural and Personal Differences**: Different cultural backgrounds, personal work styles, or even personality types can influence how feedback is given and interpreted.

As a feedback giver, understanding the root causes of the conflict will help you handle the situation with more empathy and clarity.

Example: Imagine a team member receives feedback from their supervisor that they need to improve their communication skills with clients, but a peer suggests that they need to focus more on technical expertise. Both pieces of feedback are valuable, but they conflict in terms of priority and focus.

2. Acknowledge the Complexity of the Situation

When delivering feedback that is contradictory or comes from different sources, it's important to acknowledge the complexity of the situation. This not only shows that you understand the recipient's struggle but also sets the stage for a constructive conversation.

Coaching Tips for Acknowledging Complexity:

- **Validate the Experience**: Start by acknowledging that receiving contradictory feedback can be confusing. Make sure the recipient understands that it's okay to feel uncertain about how to move forward.
- **Empathy and Reassurance**: Reassure them that the feedback does not necessarily negate one another. Different people may have different focuses or areas of concern. Your role is to help them navigate these differences.

Example: "I understand that you've received feedback from different people, and it may feel like they're pointing you in different directions. That's common, and it's part of working in a collaborative environment. Let's work together to sort this out."

3. Clarifying the Feedback

Before you can help the recipient turn conflicting feedback into actionable steps, it's essential to clarify exactly what each piece of feedback means. In some cases, feedback may be vague or general, which only adds to the confusion. As a feedback giver, it's important to help the recipient break down the feedback into understandable, specific components.

Coaching Tips for Clarification:

- **Ask for Specifics**: Encourage the recipient to ask for specific examples if the feedback they've received is unclear. This allows them to better understand the feedback and avoid misunderstandings.

- **Contextualize the Feedback**: Help them understand the context in which the feedback was given. Ask them to consider the perspective of the person delivering the feedback, such as their role, priorities, and motivations.

- **Reframe the Feedback**: In cases where feedback seems contradictory, work with the recipient to reframe it. This could involve recognizing that feedback can apply to different contexts or audiences.

Example: "Let's break this down. When your supervisor said you need to improve communication, what exactly do you think they meant? Were they referring to written communication, meetings, or one-on-one discussions? That will help you determine what actions to take."

4. Identifying Overarching Themes and Priorities

Often, contradictory feedback highlights different priorities or different perspectives. Your job as the feedback giver is to help the recipient identify any overarching themes, and determine which feedback should take priority based on their goals and current needs.

Coaching Tips for Identifying Themes:

- **Look for Patterns**: Encourage the recipient to identify common threads between the feedback they've received. Do multiple sources mention similar areas for improvement, even if they're framed differently?

- **Clarify Current Priorities**: Help the recipient align the feedback with their personal and professional goals. Are the priorities related to current tasks, long-term development, or a specific project? If the feedback focuses on different areas (e.g., time management vs. communication), help them prioritize based on what will drive the most immediate value.

Example: If one feedback source emphasizes communication skills, and another focuses on technical skills, ask the recipient to reflect on what is most pressing for their current role or upcoming project. "Which of these areas will help you achieve the goals you've set for yourself this quarter?"

5. Making a Decision: How to Integrate Conflicting Feedback into Actionable Plans

Once the conflicting feedback has been clarified and the themes identified, the next step is to help the recipient decide on a course of action. Often, the best course of action involves integrating multiple pieces of feedback into a comprehensive development plan. It's important to work with the recipient to find a balanced approach that acknowledges all perspectives.

Coaching Tips for Integration:

- **Create a Balanced Action Plan**: Help the recipient integrate both pieces of feedback into a balanced, actionable plan. For example, if one piece of feedback is about improving communication with clients and another is about developing technical skills, help them identify how they can work on both, without one overwhelming the other.

- **Offer Guidance on Sequencing**: If feedback is contradictory in terms of immediate action, work with the recipient to determine a logical order for addressing both sets of feedback. Sometimes, one area of improvement needs to be tackled first before the other.

- **Set Milestones and Reassess**: When there are competing pieces of feedback, it's useful to set short-term milestones to track progress on both fronts. Regular check-ins allow the recipient to reassess their priorities and adapt the plan as necessary.

Example: "We've identified that improving your communication and technical skills are both priorities. Let's start by focusing on communication for the next month. Once we see improvement in that area, we can start integrating more technical learning. How does that sound?"

6. Using Feedback as a Continuous Learning Process

One of the most important lessons in handling conflicting feedback is to view it as an ongoing process rather than a one-time event. Feedback, especially when it is contradictory, provides valuable insights into areas for growth. It also highlights the complexity of real-world work environments, where there is no one-size-fits-all approach to success.

Coaching Tips for Continuous Learning:

- **Embrace Feedback as a Growth Opportunity**: Encourage the recipient to see feedback, even when contradictory, as a sign of the diverse perspectives at play. Emphasize that feedback is a tool for continual learning, not an indication of failure.

- **Foster a Growth Mindset**: Cultivate a mindset of resilience and curiosity in the recipient. Teach them that learning to navigate conflicting feedback is part of professional development and is something to embrace.

- **Encourage Reflection and Adjustment**: Regularly encourage the recipient to reflect on their progress, adjusting their strategies and actions as new feedback comes in. This promotes an iterative process of growth.

Example: "Remember, feedback is just one part of the learning process. As you implement these changes, continue seeking feedback to refine your approach."

Navigating conflicting feedback is an inevitable part of professional and personal growth. By acknowledging the complexity, clarifying the feedback, identifying overarching themes, and integrating it into actionable plans, you can help your recipients turn confusion into clarity and opportunity. The goal is not to give them a simple answer, but to empower them to navigate feedback with confidence and use it to drive improvement.

Chapter 11

Overcoming Defensiveness: Delivering Feedback to Resistant Recipients

One of the most challenging situations when giving negative feedback is encountering defensiveness or resistance from the recipient. Whether due to insecurity, pride, or simply a natural reaction to criticism, defensiveness can derail a feedback conversation and prevent meaningful change. Understanding how to manage these moments with care can make the difference between a defensive exchange and a productive discussion.

1. Recognizing the Signs of Defensiveness

Before diving into strategies for delivering feedback to a defensive recipient, it's crucial to first understand what defensiveness looks like. Recognizing the signs of defensiveness early in the feedback conversation allows you to adjust your approach and manage the interaction more effectively.

Common Signs of Defensiveness:

- **Denial or Blame**: The recipient may deny the issue or deflect blame onto others, rather than accepting responsibility.

- **Interrupting or Over-explaining**: When people are defensive, they might interrupt your feedback or provide excessive justifications for their behaviour.

- **Emotional Responses**: Defensiveness can manifest as anger, frustration, or even tearfulness. These reactions can stem from feeling personally attacked or misunderstood.

- **Withdrawal or Silence**: In some cases, the person may shut down emotionally or mentally, becoming disengaged or silent in response to your feedback.

Coaching Tip for Recognizing Defensiveness:

As a feedback giver, it's important not to take these signs personally. Often, defensiveness is a coping mechanism rather than an intentional reaction to you. Your role is to stay calm and focused on helping the individual move past their initial reaction.

Example: "I notice that you seem upset right now. It's okay, let's take a moment and approach this together so that we can make this a constructive conversation."

2. Creating a Safe and Respectful Environment

A key part of reducing defensiveness is ensuring that the feedback environment feels safe and respectful. When the recipient feels that their dignity is being respected, they are more likely to remain open to feedback, even if it's negative.

Coaching Tips for Creating a Safe Environment:

- **Private and Respectful Setting**: Always deliver negative feedback in a private setting where the individual doesn't feel exposed or humiliated. Public feedback, especially negative feedback, can lead to feelings of shame, which often triggers defensiveness.

- **Use a Positive, Collaborative Tone**: Begin by affirming the recipient's strengths and contributions. Frame your feedback as an opportunity for improvement rather than a criticism. This sets a more collaborative tone for the conversation.

- **Maintain Body Language Awareness**: Non-verbal cues are just as important as the words you speak. Maintain an open and non-confrontational posture. Avoid crossing your arms or using an aggressive tone of voice, as these can escalate defensiveness.

Example: "I want to make sure you understand that my goal is to help you improve. We're in this together, and I believe in your ability to make changes. Let's talk about how we can approach this constructively."

3. Stay Calm and Focused on the Issue, Not the Person

When delivering negative feedback, particularly to someone who is defensive, it's essential to remain calm and focus on the behaviour, not the person. Attacking someone's character or making overly harsh judgments can make the recipient feel personally attacked, which exacerbates their defensiveness.

Coaching Tips for Keeping the Focus on Behaviour:

- **Use "I" Statements**: Rather than saying, "You always make mistakes" or "You never follow through," try saying, "I noticed that in this particular instance, the follow-up was missed." This makes the feedback feel less accusatory.
- **Describe, Don't Label**: Stick to specific behaviours and outcomes, rather than labelling the person. Instead of calling someone "lazy" or "incompetent," focus on the specific actions they can improve.
- **Be Solution-Oriented**: Once you've addressed the issue, shift the conversation toward solutions. Discuss how the recipient can improve and what steps they can take moving forward.

Example: "In our last meeting, I felt the discussion was a bit disorganized. It led to some confusion among the team about next steps. How do you think we could approach it differently in the future?"

4. Use Active Listening to Validate Their Emotions

Defensive reactions are often rooted in emotions, such as fear, shame, or frustration. One of the most effective ways to manage defensiveness is to validate those emotions by actively listening and acknowledging their feelings before continuing with the feedback process.

Coaching Tips for Active Listening:

- **Empathetic Responses**: Acknowledge the emotional aspect of the conversation by reflecting back what you hear. For example, "I can see this is frustrating for you" or "I understand that this feedback might feel difficult to hear."

- **Ask Clarifying Questions**: Give the recipient space to explain their point of view. Clarifying questions help you to understand their perspective, while also making them feel heard and understood.
- **Remain Non-Judgmental**: Avoid jumping to conclusions or interrupting. Allow the recipient to express their feelings fully before you respond.

Example: "It seems like this situation has upset you, and I want to understand more about how you see things. Can you share your thoughts on what led to this?"

5. Reframing Negative Feedback as a Growth Opportunity

To reduce defensiveness, help the recipient view the feedback as an opportunity for growth rather than as an attack. When people understand that feedback is about improvement, not punishment, they are more likely to engage with it constructively.

Coaching Tips for Reframing Feedback:

- **Focus on the Future**: Frame the conversation around what the recipient can do moving forward. Rather than dwelling on past mistakes, emphasize what actions can be taken to make improvements.
- **Highlight Their Strengths**: Reinforce the recipient's value and contributions before diving into the areas that need improvement. This balanced approach can make them feel less threatened by the negative feedback.
- **Collaborative Problem-Solving**: Approach the conversation as a team effort. Ask the recipient what steps they think could help them improve, making them an active participant in the solution.

Example: "I know you've done a great job on the recent project, and I think you can build on that. Let's talk about some ways to refine your communication with the team so we can avoid confusion in the future."

6. Encourage Reflection and Follow-Up

The feedback conversation doesn't end once you've delivered your message. Defensiveness can sometimes be a delayed reaction, so it's important to provide follow-up opportunities to revisit the feedback and assess progress. This gives the recipient a chance to reflect on the feedback at their own pace and ask for clarification if necessary.

Coaching Tips for Follow-Up:

- **Schedule Check-Ins**: Offer to revisit the topic in the future to gauge progress. This shows that you're invested in their development and creates an opportunity to adjust your approach if needed.

- **Encourage Self-Reflection**: Ask the recipient to reflect on the feedback on their own time. Give them space to process and internalize the conversation before asking them to take action.

Example: "Let's plan to check in next month to see how things are going. In the meantime, take some time to think about what we discussed and feel free to come to me with any questions."

Dealing with defensiveness when delivering feedback is a delicate but essential skill. By recognizing the signs of defensiveness early on, creating a safe and respectful environment, staying calm and solution-focused, and validating the recipient's emotions, you can turn a potentially difficult conversation into a productive one. With patience and empathy, you can help individuals overcome their initial resistance and transform negative feedback into an opportunity for growth.

Chapter 12

Cultivating a Culture: Building Environments Where Negative Feedback is Welcomed

The ability to give and receive negative feedback effectively is a critical skill for personal and professional growth. But it's not just about individual interactions; to truly thrive in a feedback-rich environment, we must build a culture where feedback—both positive and negative—is welcomed, embraced, and used constructively.

1. The Importance of a Feedback Culture

A feedback culture isn't just about having regular feedback conversations; it's about fostering an environment where feedback is normalized, seen as a tool for improvement, and actively sought out. When feedback is a routine part of workplace or personal growth interactions, it reduces defensiveness, increases trust, and allows individuals and teams to continuously improve.

Why a Feedback Culture Matters:

- **Encourages Openness**: A strong feedback culture encourages open dialogue, making it easier for both employees and managers to discuss performance, expectations, and growth areas.

- **Promotes Learning**: Regular, constructive feedback helps people identify areas of improvement and continuously learn, contributing to overall productivity and development.

- **Builds Trust and Relationships**: When feedback is consistently delivered in a respectful, solution-oriented way, it builds trust between individuals and teams. People feel supported and valued, rather than criticized.

- **Drives Continuous Improvement**: A feedback-oriented environment promotes a growth mindset, where everyone is invested in developing and performing better over time.

Example: In companies with a feedback culture, employees routinely ask for feedback, both from peers and supervisors. It's seen as a sign of maturity and professional development, rather than as a reaction to mistakes or failures.

2. Leading by Example: How to Model Constructive Feedback

To build a culture where feedback is welcomed, leadership must set the tone. Leaders and managers play a critical role in establishing and modelling constructive feedback practices. When leaders consistently give feedback in a respectful, balanced, and growth-oriented way, it encourages others to do the same.

Coaching Tips for Leaders:

- **Be Transparent and Vulnerable**: Share your own experiences of receiving feedback. Demonstrating that you, too, are open to feedback helps normalize the process.

- **Model Feedback Practices**: Regularly provide constructive feedback to your team, showing them how to balance praise with areas for improvement.

- **Solicit Feedback from Others**: Actively seek feedback from others, especially those who report to you. This demonstrates that feedback is a two-way street and can be used for personal growth at all levels.

Example: A manager who actively asks their team, "What can I do to help you more effectively?" or "What could I improve on as a leader?" not only shows humility but also reinforces the idea that feedback is an essential tool for development.

3. Creating Safe Spaces for Feedback

One of the biggest barriers to a feedback culture is the fear of criticism. If people feel that giving or receiving feedback could have negative consequences—such as damaging relationships or hindering career advancement—they will avoid the conversation altogether. This is why it's essential to create safe spaces where feedback can be shared openly without fear of retaliation or judgment.

Coaching Tips for Creating Safety:

- **Ensure Anonymity When Needed**: Allow employees or peers to give feedback anonymously if they feel uncomfortable doing so openly. This can help alleviate fears of confrontation and retaliation.

- **Encourage a Growth-Oriented Mindset**: Make sure that feedback conversations are framed as opportunities for growth, not punishment. This mindset reduces defensiveness and encourages people to engage more willingly.

- **Set Ground Rules for Feedback**: Create clear guidelines for feedback that emphasize respect, tact, and the focus on behaviours rather than personal traits. Setting expectations ahead of time helps reduce anxiety.

Example: In team meetings, ensure everyone knows that constructive criticism will be handled respectfully, and that feedback should always aim to solve problems, not point fingers.

4. Training for Feedback Skills

Building a feedback culture doesn't happen overnight. It requires consistent training and development to ensure that all members of the organization have the necessary skills to both give and receive feedback constructively. Without these skills, feedback can be misinterpreted, delivered poorly, or avoided altogether.

Coaching Tips for Feedback Training:

- **Offer Feedback Workshops**: Organize workshops or training sessions that focus on teaching feedback skills, such as active listening, delivering feedback with empathy, and receiving feedback without defensiveness.

- **Use Real-Life Examples**: Incorporate real-life case studies or examples into training sessions, showing both good and bad feedback practices. This helps participants understand the nuances of feedback and how it can impact relationships and performance.

- **Encourage Peer-to-Peer Feedback**: Create opportunities for peer-to-peer feedback, which can be less intimidating than feedback from managers. Peer feedback also helps build team cohesion and mutual respect.

Example: A company might host a monthly "feedback exchange" session where employees practice giving and receiving feedback in a low-pressure environment, using role-playing exercises.

5. Overcoming Resistance to Feedback

Resistance to feedback is a common challenge, especially in environments where feedback is not the norm. Employees may be unfamiliar with the process, have had negative experiences in the past, or feel insecure about their performance. Overcoming this resistance requires patience, empathy, and consistent reinforcement of feedback's value.

Coaching Tips for Overcoming Resistance:

- **Normalize Feedback**: Reinforce that feedback is a normal and necessary part of the development process. The more it's integrated into everyday activities, the less intimidating it becomes.

- **Provide Positive Reinforcement**: When someone responds positively to feedback or asks for it willingly, offer praise. This reinforces the behaviour and encourages others to embrace feedback.

- **Offer Continuous Support**: Provide ongoing support to those who are resistant to feedback. Regular follow-up conversations can help them see that feedback is a helpful tool for improvement, not a personal attack.

Example: A team member who initially resists feedback might eventually come around when they see that feedback leads to real improvements in their performance and relationships.

6. Measuring and Tracking Feedback Success

To know if a feedback culture is truly taking hold, organizations need to track the success of their feedback efforts. This involves collecting data on feedback frequency, feedback effectiveness, and employee satisfaction with the feedback process.

Coaching Tips for Measuring Feedback Success:

- **Conduct Surveys and Gather Input**: Use surveys or informal feedback to gauge how employees feel about the feedback culture. Ask questions like, "Do you feel comfortable giving and receiving feedback?" and "Has feedback led to improvements in your work?"

- **Monitor Behavioural Changes**: Pay attention to changes in performance, collaboration, and communication as a result of regular feedback. Improvements in these areas can indicate that the feedback culture is becoming more ingrained.

- **Adjust Strategies Based on Results**: Use the feedback you receive from employees about the feedback process to adjust your approach. Continually refine how feedback is given and received to ensure it remains effective.

Example: An organization might track the frequency of feedback conversations, employee engagement with feedback, and changes in performance metrics to assess the success of their feedback culture.

Building a culture where feedback is not only accepted but actively sought out is essential for organizational success. By leading by example, creating safe spaces for feedback, providing consistent training, and measuring progress, you can cultivate an environment where feedback becomes a natural and integral part of professional development. When everyone in the organization views feedback as a tool for growth, it transforms how teams collaborate, innovate, and thrive.

Bibliography

- **American Institute of Stress**. (2018). The Benefits of Deep Breathing. Retrieved from stress.org.
- **Brown, B.** (2012). *Daring Greatly: How the Courage to Be Vulnerable Transforms the Way We Live, Love, Parent, and Lead*. Gotham Books.
- **Brown, B.** (2018). *Dare to Lead: Brave Work. Tough Conversations. Whole Hearts*. Random House.
- **Cacioppo, J. T., & Patrick, W.** (2008). *Loneliness: Human Nature and the Need for Social Connection*. W.W. Norton & Company.
- **Carver, C. S., & Scheier, M. F.** (1998). *On the Self-Regulation of Behaviour*. Cambridge University Press.
- **Centre for Creative Leadership**. (2016). The Importance of Dialogue in Feedback. Leadership Insights Series.
- **Centre for Creative Leadership**. (2020). Feedback That Works: How to Build and Deliver Your Message. Retrieved from ccl.org.
- **Clark, C.** (2017). *The 5 Levels of Leadership: Proven Steps to Maximize Your Potential*. Centre Street.
- **Covey, S. R.** (1989). *The 7 Habits of Highly Effective People: Powerful Lessons in Personal Change*. Free Press.
- **Covey, S. M. R.** (2006). *The Speed of Trust: The One Thing That Changes Everything*. Free Press.
- **Dweck, C. S.** (2006). *Mindset: The New Psychology of Success*. Random House.
- **Edmondson, A. C.** (2018). *The Fearless Organization: Creating Psychological Safety in the Workplace for Learning, Innovation, and Growth*. Wiley.
- **Ed. William, H. M.** (2019). *Resolving Conflicts: A Guide to Successful Conflict Resolution Strategies*. Routledge.
- **Goleman, D.** (1998). *Working with Emotional Intelligence*. Bantam.
- **Goleman, D.** (2006). *Emotional Intelligence: Why It Can Matter More Than IQ*. Bantam Books.
- **Goldsmith, M.** (2002). *What Got You Here Won't Get You There: How Successful People Become Even More Successful*. Hyperion.
- **Goldsmith, M.** (2009). *What Got You Here Won't Get You There: How Successful People Become Even More Successful*. Hyperion.

- **Google Re.** (2016). Guide: Understand Team Effectiveness. Google's Project Aristotle.
- **Gottman, J., & Silver, N.** (1999). *The Seven Principles for Making Marriage Work*. Harmony Books.
- **Grant, A.** (2016). *Originals: How Non-Conformists Move the World*. Viking.
- **Gross, J. J.** (1998). The Emerging Field of Emotion Regulation: An Integrative Review. *Review of General Psychology, 2*(3), 271–299.
- **Harvard Business Review.** (2014). The Art of Asking Questions. Retrieved from Harvard Business Review.
- **Hattie, J., & Timperley, H.** (2007). The Power of Feedback. *Review of Educational Research, 77*(1), 81-112.
- **Heen, S., & Stone, D.** (2014). *Thanks for the Feedback: The Science and Art of Receiving Feedback Well*. Penguin Books.
- **IBM HR Reports**. (2019). Case Study on Employee Feedback and Satisfaction. Internal Publication.
- **International Journal of Listening**. (2015). The Impact of Active Listening on Employee Engagement and Productivity.
- **Journal of Applied Psychology**. (2017). The Role of Breaks in High-Stress Conversations.
- **Journal of Communication**. (2015). The Impact of "I" Statements in Reducing Defensiveness in Communication.
- **Kabat-Zinn, J.** (1990). *Full Catastrophe Living: Using the Wisdom of Your Body and Mind to Face Stress, Pain, and Illness*. Delacorte.
- **Keirsey, D.** (1998). *Please Understand Me II: Temperament, Character, Intelligence*. Prometheus Nemesis.
- **Kluger, A. N., & DeNisi, A.** (1996). The Effects of Feedback Interventions on Performance: A Historical Review and a Meta-Analysis. *Psychological Bulletin*.
- **Kohn, A.** (2015). *Punished by Rewards: The Trouble with Gold Stars, Incentive Plans, A's, Praise, and Other Bribes*. Houghton Mifflin Harcourt.
- **Lieberman, M. D.** (2013). *Social: Why Our Brains Are Wired to Connect*. Crown Publishers.
- **MindTools**. (2021). How to Handle Criticism at Work. MindTools.
- **Mehrabian, A.** (1971). *Silent Messages: Implicit Communication of Emotions and Attitudes*. Wadsworth Publishing.
- **Rock, D.** (2006). SCARF: A Brain-Based Model for Collaborating with and Influencing Others. Neuro Leadership Institute.

- **Rock, D.** (2008). *Your Brain at Work: Strategies for Overcoming Distraction, Regaining Focus, and Working Smarter All Day Long.* Harper Business.
- **Rogers, C. R.** (1951). *Client-Centred Therapy: Its Current Practice, Implications, and Theory.* Houghton Mifflin.
- **Rosenberg, M. B.** (2003). *Nonviolent Communication: A Language of Life.* Puddle Dancer Press.
- **Schein, E. H.** (2010). *Organizational Culture and Leadership.* Jossey-Bass.
- **Siegel, D. J.** (2012). *The Whole-Brain Child: 12 Revolutionary Strategies to Nurture Your Child's Developing Mind.* Delacorte.
- **Skinner, B. F.** (1953). *Science and Human Behaviour.* Free Press.
- **Stone, D., & Heen, S.** (2014). *Thanks for the Feedback: The Science and Art of Receiving Feedback Well.* Penguin Books.
- **Sutton, R. I.** (2007). *The No Asshole Rule: Building a Civilized Workplace and Surviving One That Isn't.* Business Plus.
- **Tannen, D.** (1990). *You Just Don't Understand: Women and Men in Conversation.* Ballantine Books.

About the Author

Ben Sorensen is, amongst other things, a curious neurodiverse research author whose writings are about sparking curiosity, providing useful tools, and expanding minds!

Aside from writing, Ben is also an Australian personality who hosts events, is a keynote speaker, a red carpet regular, voiceover artist and happens to also have Autism and ADHD.

Read more at bensorensen1.com

www.ingramcontent.com/pod-product-compliance
Lightning Source LLC
Chambersburg PA
CBHW071109240526
45469CB00006BD/2405